D1412132

small worlds

ON THE TUNDRA

Jen Green

CRABTREE
Publishing Company
www.crabtreebooks.com

Crabtree Publishing Company
www.crabtreebooks.com

PMB 16A, 350 Fifth Avenue
Suite 3308
New York, NY 10118

612 Welland Avenue
St. Catharines
Ontario L2M 5V6

CRABTREE:
Project editor: P. A. Finlay
Assistant editor: Carrie Gleason
Coordinating editor: Ellen Rodger

BROWN PARTWORKS:
Editor: Amanda Harman
Designer: Joan Curtis
Picture researcher: Susannah Jayes
Managing editor: Bridget Giles
Commissioning editor: Anne O'Daly
Consultants: Robert G. White, PhD, Professor Emeritus (Director Emeritus),
University of Alaska Fairbanks, Institute of Arctic Biology
David T. Brown, PhD, Center for the Environment, Brock University

Illustrator: Peter Bull
Photographs: Edwin & Peggy Bauer/Bruce Coleman Collection p 29; Steven C. Kaufman/Bruce
Coleman Collection p 25; Johnny Johnson/Bruce Coleman Collection pp 7t, 16t, 21b; Wayne Lankinen/
Bruce Coleman Collection p 24t; Joe McDonald/Bruce Coleman Collection p 21t; Dr. Eckart Pott/
Bruce Coleman Collection p 27b; John Shaw/Bruce Coleman Collection p 16m; Jorg & Petra Wegner/
Bruce Coleman Collection p 4; Staffan Widstrand/Bruce Coleman Collection p 17; Wolfgang Kaehler/Corbis
p 31; B. & C. Alexander/NHPA, front and back cover, pp 5, 8m, 10, 15; Laurie Campbell/NHPA pp 18t, 30;
Manfred Danegger/NHPA p 19 inset; Hellio & Van Ingen/NHPA p 23; Rich Kirchner/NHPA, front cover b/r,
title page, pp 24m, 27t; T. Kitchin & V. Hurst/NHPA pp 19, 26; Stephen Krasemann/NHPA pp 13, 20; Gerard
Lacz/NHPA p 6; David Middleton/NHPA p 3, 8t; John Shaw/NHPA pp 9, 11; Mirko Stelzner/NHPA p 7m, 12;
Alan Williams/NHPA p 28; Werner Zepf/NHPA p 147m, 12; Alan Williams/NHPA p 28; Werner Zepf/
NHPA p 14, Hubert Klein/ Still Pictures p18b

Created and produced by
Brown Partworks Limited

First edition
10 9 8 7 6 5 4 3 2 1
Copyright © 2002 Brown Partworks Limited
Printed in Singapore

CATALOGING-IN-PUBLICATION DATA

Green, Jen.
  On the tundra / Jen Green.-- 1st ed.
    p. cm. -- (Small worlds)
  Summary: Describes the harsh conditions of the tundra, as well as the kinds of plants and
animals that can flourish there.
    ISBN 0-7787-0139-5 (rlb)-- ISBN 0-7787-0153-0 (pbk.)
    1. Tundra ecology--Juvenile literature. 2. Tundras--Juvenile literature. [1. Tundra ecology. 2.
Ecology. 3. Tundras.] I. Title II. Series: Small worlds (New York, N.Y.)
  QH541.5.T8 G75 2002
  577.5'86--dc21
                        2001047524
                        LC

Contents

Tundra around the world

In the far north of our planet lies a cold land called the tundra. Despite the harsh conditions, many plants and animals live there.

▲ *The lynx's habitat sometimes stretches onto the tundra. In winter, its light gray spotted coat blends in well with the snowy landscape.*

The tundra is a belt of treeless lowlands that is **circumpolar** because it follows the **Arctic Circle** and extends around the entire globe. The Arctic Ocean lies north of the tundra and is covered by thick ice. The taiga, a belt of **coniferous** trees, lies south of the tundra.

This book introduces the plants and animals that live on and around the North American tundra. Similar **species** live in Scandinavia in northern Europe, and Siberia in Arctic Russia.

▶ *A layer of frozen ground, called permafrost, lies under the top layer of soil on the tundra. In summer, the snow and ice melt. Meltwater cannot drain through the permafrost, so it collects on the surface, forming many marshes, lakes, and pools.*

▶ *The tundra (in red) stretches across North America, Europe, and Siberia, in and around the Arctic Circle (dotted line).*

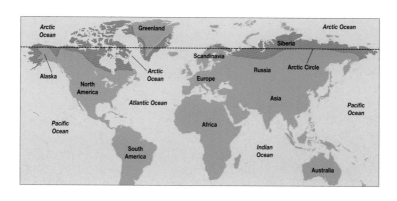

4

Life on the Tundra

polar bear

muskox

snowy owl

wolf

peregrine falcon

Some animals make the tundra their permanent home because they can survive the freezing winters. Others stay for the summer and migrate south for the winter.

As Earth moves around the Sun, it tilts on an **axis**. When the North Pole leans toward the Sun, it is summer on the tundra, and there is almost 24 hours of daylight. In winter, when the North Pole tilts away from the Sun, the tundra is dark.

Year-round residents

Animals that live on the southern tundra all year include mammals such as the Arctic fox and birds such as the ptarmigan and gyrfalcon (below).

ptarmigan

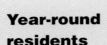
Arctic hare

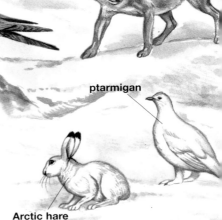
Arctic fox

weasel

vole

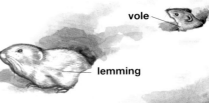
lemming

crane

Arctic tern

Summer visitors

Animals, such as geese, cranes, grizzly bears, moose, and some caribou, can survive the tundra only in the summer.

grizzly bear

moose

lynx

Tough plants and insects

Tundra plants are tough enough to withstand freezing winters and shallow soil. Mosses and flowering plants grow close to the ground, away from icy winds. Many insects, including butterflies, survive on the tundra.

caribou

wolverine

Arctic willow

Arctic lupin

Arctic poppy

snow goose

curlew

midges and gnats

mosquito

lichens

Plants and insects

Hundreds of different plants and insects live on the tundra. They can survive the long months of darkness and bitter cold of an Arctic winter.

▲ *When summer comes to the tundra, plants burst into flower and the sound of buzzing insects fills the air.*

▶ *Dwarf trees, such as this Arctic willow, produce large flowers that attract insects, especially bees and moths.*

Only dwarf varieties of trees, such as willow and birch, survive on the open tundra. Instead of growing upward, these miniature trees grow more like shrubs, spreading their branches along the ground, out of the wind. Their tiny trunks may measure only a few inches across even when fully grown.

▶ *No tall trees grow on the tundra. The dark spruce and fir trees thin out at the edge of the taiga.*

Keeping warm

Plants, such as purple saxifrage and moss campion, grow in low, dense groups. In winter, these herbs escape the killing frosts under a protective blanket of snow. Like many other flowering plants that bloom on the tundra, Arctic poppies cover south-facing slopes or grow in sheltered hollows, away from the howling winds.

▲ Purple saxifrage is a small, low-growing herb. It starts growing at the first rays of spring sunshine and flowers even before the snow has melted.

Collecting light and water

Like almost all plants everywhere, tundra plants use their roots to anchor themselves in the soil and to collect moisture and minerals. The roots of tundra plants cannot penetrate the rock-solid **permafrost**, so they have shallow roots that fan out horizontally, gathering moisture from the thin topsoil. Like all plants, they use the process of **photosynthesis** to make their own food, using the energy in sunlight.

▶ Arctic poppies have tiny hairs on their stems and leaves. These trap the sun's heat.

Small, dark leaves absorb sunlight quickly. Some plants angle their leaves to catch the low, slanting rays of the sun and are able to photosynthesize even in dim light.

The growing season

All tundra plants have a very short growing season. In the northern tundra, this season lasts for only about eight weeks in July and August, when daytime temperatures rise above freezing. Most Arctic plants are **perennial**—they live for many years but do all their growing in summer. Other plants, such as poppies, are **annuals**. They sprout from seeds blown by the wind. Then, they flower, produce seeds, and die in just one season.

FANTASTIC FACTS

● Dwarf willows measure just four inches (ten centimeters) tall, but their branches stretch sixteen feet (five meters) along the ground.

● Even when they are several hundred years old, their trunks may be less than an inch (one or two centimeters) across.

▼ *These Arctic lupins are perennial plants that grow and bloom quickly every summer.*

FANTASTIC FACTS

● In the tundra, summer daytime temperatures range from 32 to 50°F (0 to 10°C). In winter, temperatures may fall as low as −40°F (−40°C).

● The plains of the tundra receive less than fifteen inches (38 cm) of rain each year on average.

In summer, the tundra is a blaze of colors, with pink, purple, and yellow flowers carpeting the ground.

In the far north, only mosses, lichens, and some grasses can survive the very harsh conditions. Mosses grow in dense, soggy mats that cover the ground. Lichens are made up of two living things—**fungi** and **algae**. Each depends on the other for survival. The fungi provide shelter and moisture for the algae, which photosynthesize to make food.

▼ *Some lichens are low growing and cover the surface of rocks.*

Wet and dry

Drought is a problem on some areas of the tundra. The air is cold and dry and little rain falls. For these reasons, the tundra is also called a polar desert. Tundra plants in these regions suck every drop of precious moisture from the bone-dry ground. Other areas are swampy, because water cannot drain through the frozen permafrost. Marsh plants such as heathers, mosses, and cranberries (shown below) flourish.

Some lichens grow on stones and boulders. Other lichens grow in thick mats. One of these, called reindeer moss, is a yellow lichen that looks like thousands of tiny reindeer antlers. It provides nourishment for animals, such as caribou, in winter when other food is scarce.

Tundra animals

Insects and other small animals,
such as spiders, also live on the
tundra. Arctic insects include flies,
beetles, moths, and butterflies.
Unlike warm-blooded birds and
mammals, these animals are cold-
blooded. This means that to keep
warm they have to take heat from
their surroundings, and to keep cool
they lose heat to their surroundings.
In freezing weather, small animals
from warmer lands cannot stay active,
yet tundra species can.

▶ *The southern
tundra is home to
many beautiful
butterflies. Their life
cycles take
years to
complete
because of
the short
summers.*

Arctic survival

The blood of some tundra insects contains a substance that prevents them from freezing. Many other insects on the tundra have dark-colored bodies that absorb heat from the sun quicker than pale colors do. Some species are covered with fine hairs that trap heat and provide insulation.

The life cycles of tundra animals coincide with the tundra seasons. These insects hatch, grow, and breed in the short months of spring and summer. They lay tough-shelled eggs that survive the winter and hatch the next spring.

▲ *Mosquitoes, midges, gnats, and blackflies are common insects around tundra pools.*

Blood-suckers and flesh-eaters

In summer, large clouds of mosquitoes descend on caribou and other warm-blooded animals to drink their blood. Their large prey provide food and warmth for the insects.

Other insects lay their eggs on their hosts. For example, botflies lay their eggs in the nasal, or nose, passages of caribou. When the maggots hatch, they burrow up into the deer's nose to feed and spend the winter in warmth and safety. Mosquito **larvae** hatch and mature in marshy pools on the tundra.

▼ *Warble flies lay their eggs on the fur of the caribou. After hatching, the maggots feed on the animal's flesh.*

Year-round residents

The tundra is a bleak, icy place in winter. Some birds and mammals live here all year, despite the bitter cold.

△ The willow ptarmigan is a ground-living bird that spends the whole year on the tundra.

▷ On the southern edge of the tundra in spring, Arctic ground squirrels emerge from a deep winter sleep called hibernation. Farther north, the weather is too cold for animals to hibernate—they would freeze to death.

Unlike insects and spiders, birds and mammals are warm-blooded animals. Food provides the fuel that keeps their bodies warm in freezing weather. Birds that spend all year on the tundra south of the Arctic Circle include snowy owls and gyrfalcons. Mammals include Arctic foxes, Peary caribou, muskoxen, lemmings, weasels, and polar bears.

▷ Muskoxen feed on tundra grasses, mosses, and lichens. They can dig out their food from under the deep snow.

The Arctic hare is the only hare to live as far north as the Arctic. It feeds on tundra plants such as Arctic willow.

Rodents, such as this collared lemming, live in snowy burrows in winter. The temperature there is much warmer than above ground.

Feathers and fur

In the fall, mammals and birds eat a lot and build up a layer of body fat that will keep them warm in winter. Birds grow a dense coat of feathers with two layers—a tough, waterproof layer of outer feathers, and a soft, warm, downy underlayer. Mammals grow a thick coat of fur with shaggy outer hairs and woolly underfur.

Muskoxen have the longest fur of any mammal. Their tough outer hair, called guard hair, can be three feet (one meter) long. This hair protects a thick, soft underwool called qiviut. Caribou, Arctic foxes, and polar bears all have hollow hairs that trap warm air.

Keeping the heat in

Arctic mammals, such as hares and foxes, have compact bodies. With their short ears and legs, they lose less heat than long-eared, long-limbed animals from warmer lands.

Arctic foxes have hairy toes that keep them warm as they pad across the snowy landscape. Ptarmigan have feathery feet for the same reason.

Winter colors

In winter, the snowy landscape offers little cover for animals to hide from prey or predators. Smaller birds and mammals grow a white winter coat of fur or feathers. This covering blends in with their surroundings, making them difficult to see. Ptarmigan have mottled brown feathers in summer but white winter plumage. Arctic foxes, hares, and weasels have brown or gray fur in summer but a pure white winter coat.

FANTASTIC FACTS

● The tail of an Arctic fox is bushier than the tails of other foxes. The Arctic fox curls its tail around it like a warm muff when it sleeps in the snow.

● In their white winter coat, weasels are called ermines. Ermines are sometimes trapped for their fur.

▼ *The weasel looks very different in summer (left) and winter (right).*

FANTASTIC FACTS

● Muskoxen are huge animals. A muskox can weigh up to 880 pounds (400 kilograms) and might stand up to five feet (one and a half meters) tall.

● Both male and female muskoxen have sharp, curved horns.

Tundra prey

Rodents such as voles and lemmings are common on the tundra. Plant buds, shoots, roots and other plant matter are popular food choices for these small animals. In summers, when plants are abundant, lemmings breed quickly, and their populations expand rapidly. Their crowded communities are suddenly revealed when the snow melts the following spring, making them easy prey for owls, falcons, and wolves.

Lemmings are the favorite prey of weasels and Arctic foxes. The foxes sometimes hunt them by leaping up and crashing down on their burrows, forcing the lemmings out. For weasels, hunting lemmings is easier. Their bodies are slim enough to fit down lemming burrows, so they can pursue their prey underground.

▼ *The Arctic fox has very good hearing. This one has heard the rustlings of a rodent under the snow and is digging it out.*

Tundra hunters

Wolves are among the top hunters of the tundra. These wily animals usually hunt in packs of eight to twenty. On a hunt, wolves creep up on caribou and single out young, isolated, or sick deer as their prey. They surround the herd and lunge forward to separate their prey from the rest of the herd. Muskoxen protect their young from wolves by forming a circle with the calves on the inside.

▲ Working together in packs, wolves are able to kill prey as large as a muskox.

◀ The polar bear is a large predator, growing to a length of nearly eight feet (two and a half meters). In spite of its large size, it is a fast runner and can catch up easily with other swift animals, such as caribou.

Chain of life

Tundra plants and animals depend on one another for food. The relationship between these animals is called a food chain (shown on the right).

lemming

All tundra plants and animals are part of the tundra **ecosystem**. Plants and lichens make their own food through photosynthesis. Herbivores such as lemmings, ptarmigan, and caribou feed on plant matter. Some plant eaters are hunted by smaller **carnivores**, such as weasels and falcons. These in turn fall prey to the top predators of the tundra—wolves and polar bears. When animals die, their bodies are eaten and broken down by insects, spiders, and tiny bacteria. This is called decomposition. Animal remains enrich the soil to help plants grow, and so the cycle comes around again.

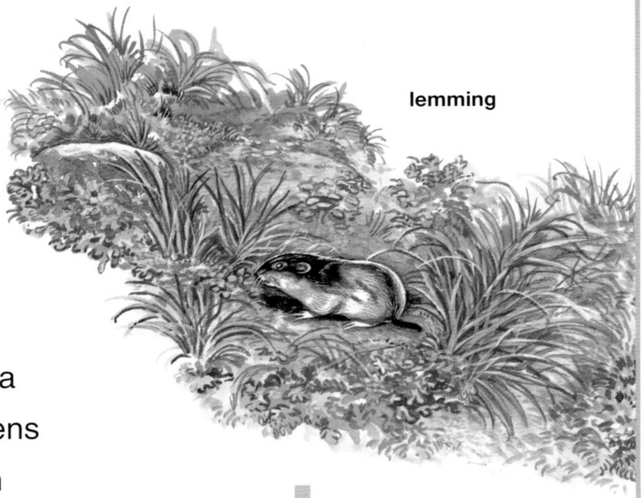

weasel

wolves

Polar bears sometimes roam the tundra, although they generally hunt on the coasts and far out on the frozen sea ice. These giant mammals are expert swimmers. They kill seals, fish, and land mammals with their sharp teeth and powerful paws.

Tundra birds

Only a handful of bird species are hardy enough to last all winter on the tundra. Ptarmigan scratch for seeds and buds under the snow with their beaks and feathery feet. Ravens are scavengers that eat any scraps of meat they come across in winter. In summer, they raid other birds' nests to steal their eggs and chicks.

Gyrfalcons and snowy owls are year-round predators in parts of the tundra where there is enough sunlight for hunting. They swoop low and seize small mammals with their sharp, hooked claws. In spring, snowy owls raise their chicks on a diet of lemmings. In years when lemming numbers are high, each owl may be healthy enough to raise up to eight chicks, but when lemmings are scarce, the owls may not breed at all.

FANTASTIC FACTS

● In winter, small birds called redpolls and buntings search for seeds on the southern tundra.

● Ravens change the lining in their nests to keep them cool in the summer and warm in the winter.

▼ *This snowy owl has caught a lemming for its young. Unlike many owls, snowy owls hunt during the day.*

Summer visitors

In summer, when deserted marshes begin to thaw, many animals migrate to the tundra to feed and breed.

▲ *Cranes fly in to spend the summer on the tundra. They hunt fish and worms in pools and streams.*

▶ *Grizzly bears rise from their winter sleep to feast on berries, small mammals, and fish.*

Migratory animals arrive in spring to take advantage of the summer climate and food sources on the tundra. From the south, they travel many miles to breed in this remote place, far from people. On the treeless plains, animals are safer from the many predators because there is more food available to the predators.

▶ *Herds of wandering caribou roam the treeless plains of the tundra during the summer.*

In the fall, both adults and their offspring begin the long trip south again.

Summer visitors include mammals such as caribou, grizzly bears, wolverine, red foxes, and lynx. Migrating birds include ducks, geese, swans, and cranes, waders such as curlews and phalaropes, snow buntings, snowy owls, jaegers, and falcons. Migrating animals travel in herds or flocks, led by experienced adults. Young animals follow their parents, who use familiar landmarks to find the way.

▲ Wolverines are large, fierce weasels. They find good summer hunting on the tundra, when they often kill animals much larger than themselves.

The wandering caribou

Some caribou are resident in the tundra, while others are summer visitors. The barren-ground caribou are known for their long **migrations**. They spend winter in the sheltered forests of the taiga and on nearby mountainsides. In spring, they move north to their summer calving grounds, traveling across open plains and sometimes over mountains and rivers filled with ice.

Caribou calves are born on the tundra in early summer, just as the snow melts. Within minutes they are up and wobbling about on their long legs.

FANTASTIC FACTS

● Caribou herds are made up of females and their young, led by the older, experienced females.

● When moving through deep snow on migration, caribou save energy by treading in the footsteps made by other animals.

In a matter of days young caribou are strong enough to follow the herd. Female caribou spend the summer feeding on lush tundra vegetation. In the fall, females trek slowly south again with their calves and the male caribou. At this time, the adults mate. The calves are born when the caribou return to the tundra the next spring.

▲ *Moose, the world's largest deer, visit the tundra in the summer. They wade through pools and snow, feeding on willow.*

Feathered visitors

More than 100 types of birds visit the tundra in spring and summer. Some arrive in April, as the snow melts, to nest and lay their eggs on the marshes. Many species have already mated before they arrive. The rest attract their partners with courtship dances and calls.

▼ *One of the most common nesting birds seen around tundra pools is the eider duck.*

Graceful fliers

Snow geese are common tundra nesters. They are easy to identify, with their snow white bodies and black wing tips. From their winter homes in the Gulf of Mexico, the geese fly 2,000 miles (3,200 km) north to breed in the Arctic. They can be seen flying overhead in V-shaped groups when traveling to and from the tundra. The geese take turns at the tip of the V, where it takes the most energy to fly.

The American golden plover makes a great show of attracting a partner with its courtship dance.

The tundra becomes busy in the spring, with the whoops, whistles, and quacks of nesting birds. Different types of birds nest close together because they eat different foods and do not need to fight for precious morsels.

Wading birds feed on insects, while ducks and geese nibble water plants.

The chicks hatch in midsummer, when food is most abundant.

Only a few weeks remain before it is time to fly south again. Parent birds lead their young to good food or spend the long hours of daylight bringing morsels for their chicks, which grow quickly. The young birds practice the swimming and flying skills they will need for the long trip south.

The coastal marshes are home to loons and eider ducks. During the long daylight hours, these birds bob and dive in the choppy waters. As the days get shorter, the flocks fly away and the marshes are once again deserted. Hares, foxes, and other year-round tundra dwellers prepare for the long, dark winter months ahead.

FANTASTIC FACTS

● Golden eagles hunt by swooping low over the treeless plains of the tundra in summer.

● When a hunt has been successful, you may see golden eagles soaring upward with prey grasped in their claws.

▼ *Golden eagles visit the tundra to hunt hares, grouse, and lemmings.*

The tundra on your doorstep

The tundra may be far away but animals near your home can behave similarly to tundra wildlife.

Squirrels and other rodents can often be seen in the fall, gathering nuts to get them through the cold winter ahead.

Bird books and websites have details of tundra birds that spend the winter in your area or pass by on their way south. Watch for geese, swans, ducks, and other migrants overhead, and study them with binoculars. Bird guides will help you identify the species you see.

When you go out bird watching, take a notebook with you to make records. If tundra birds spend winter in your area, note the date when they first appear in the fall and the last time you see them in spring.

Animal tracks

In winter, **biologists** study tundra animals by looking at their tracks in the snow. Tracks of birds and mammals can also be found in the mud by ponds and streams at any time of year. A wildlife book will help you identify the animals that made the imprints.

If your home lies close to the routes of birds migrating to and from the tundra, you will be able to watch them flying past.

Study the tracks to see how the animals were moving—were they walking, running, or hopping along?

Like tundra wildlife, the animals in your area behave differently according to the seasons. In the fall, you can watch them preparing for winter. You will see small mammals, such as squirrels, burying nuts. Groundhogs and some other rodents hibernate in winter. Note the date when you last see the animals in the winter, and the first time they appear again in the spring.

TOP TIPS FOR BIRD WATCHERS

1 Dress in warm, waterproof clothing when you go bird watching or tracking. Always take an adult with you to keep you safe.

2 Stand still when you watch migrating birds with binoculars so you will not trip and hurt yourself.

3 Dull-colored clothing will help you get close to birds on the ground. Avoid any sudden movements that will scare the animals away.

Words to know

algae Tiny plantlike organisms.

annual A plant that completes its life cycle in a single season.

Arctic Circle An imaginary line encircling Earth a few hundred miles south of the North Pole.

axis An imaginary line that passes through Earth from the North Pole to the South Pole.

biologist A scientist who studies living things such as animals.

carnivore An animal that eats flesh.

circumpolar Surrounding or located in one of the polar regions.

coniferous Needle-leaved trees such as pines and spruces.

drought A long period of time with not enough rain.

ecosystem A community of living things.

fungi A group of living things that includes toadstools and mushrooms.

larvae An immature insect.

migration A journey made regularly by animals, such as birds or moose, to escape bad weather, find food, or reach a breeding place.

perennial A plant that continues growing for a number of years.

permafrost The permanently frozen ground that lies beneath the topsoil in very cold places.

photosynthesis How plants and algae make food using sunlight.

species A group of related animals, plants, or other living things.

Index